PIANO SOLO

Country
PIANO CLASSICS

ISBN 978-1-4950-0927-3

HAL•LEONARD® CORPORATION
7777 W. BLUEMOUND RD. P.O. BOX 13819 MILWAUKEE, WI 53213

Visit Hal Leonard Online at
www.halleonard.com

4   *Blue Eyes Crying in the Rain*

11   *Born to Lose*

8   *Could I Have This Dance*

14   *Faded Love*

18   *For the Good Times*

22   *The Gambler*

30   *Green Green Grass of Home*

34   *Have I Told You Lately That I Love You*

38   *Help Me Make It Through the Night*

42   *I Can't Stop Loving You*

27   *I'm So Lonesome I Could Cry*

46 Last Date

52 Louisiana Man

49 Make the World Go Away

56 Making Believe

60 Oh, Lonesome Me

68 Room Full of Roses

65 Tennessee Waltz

76 Today I Started Loving You Again

70 Walking the Floor Over You

74 Your Cheatin' Heart

BLUE EYES CRYING IN THE RAIN

Words and Music by
FRED ROSE

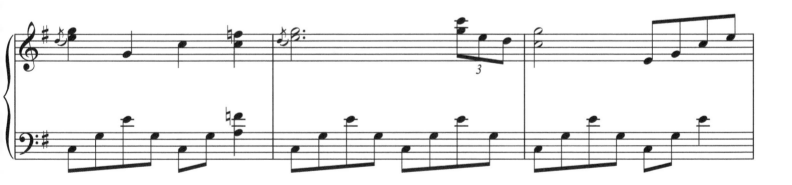

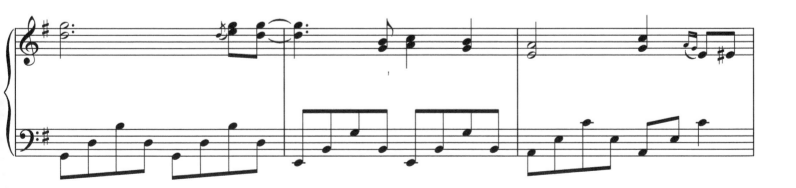

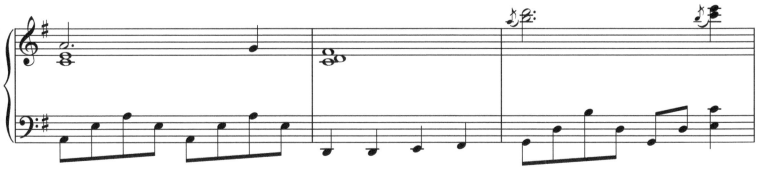

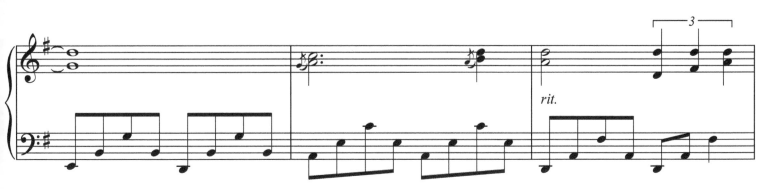

COULD I HAVE THIS DANCE
from URBAN COWBOY

Words and Music by WAYLAND HOLYFIELD
and BOB HOUSE

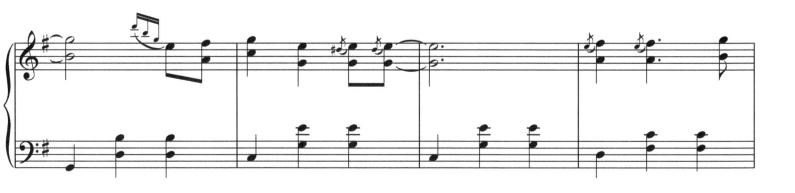

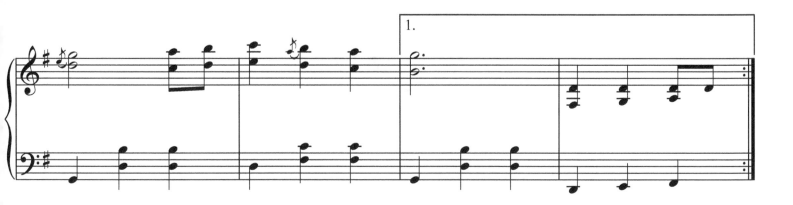

BORN TO LOSE

Words and Music by
TED DAFFAN

Moderately slow

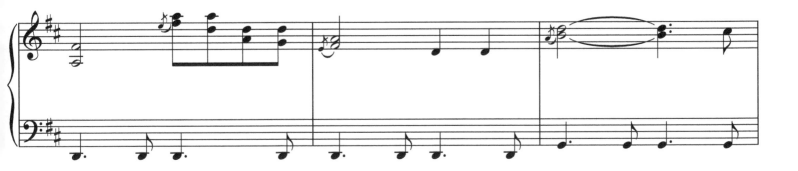

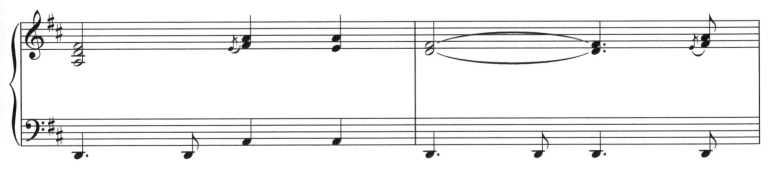

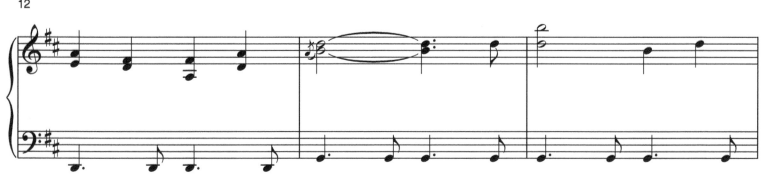

FADED LOVE

Words and Music by BOB WILLS
and JOHNNIE LEE WILLS

Brightly, in 2

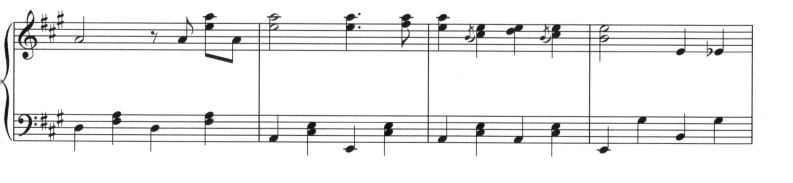

FOR THE GOOD TIMES

Words and Music by
KRIS KRISTOFFERSON

Moderately slow

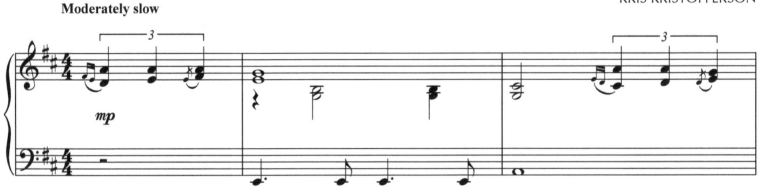

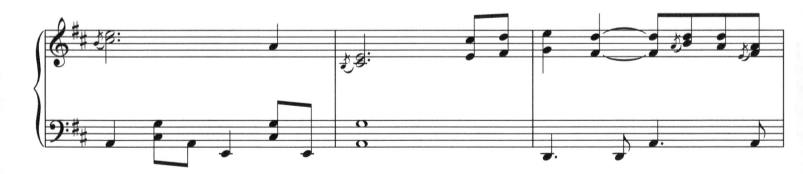

D.S. al Coda

CODA

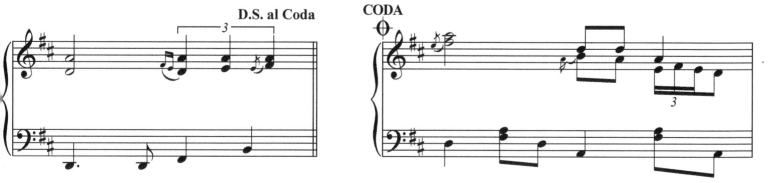

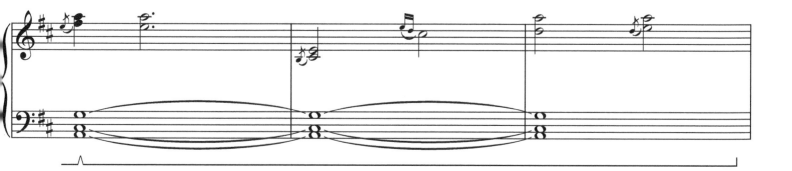

THE GAMBLER

Words and Music by
DON SCHLITZ

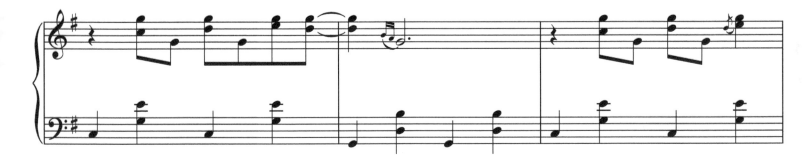

I'M SO LONESOME I COULD CRY

Words and Music by
HANK WILLIAMS

GREEN GREEN GRASS OF HOME

Words and Music by
CURLY PUTMAN

Moderately

mp

With pedal

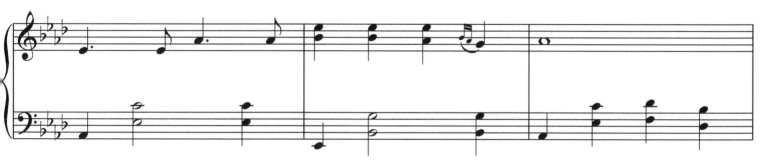

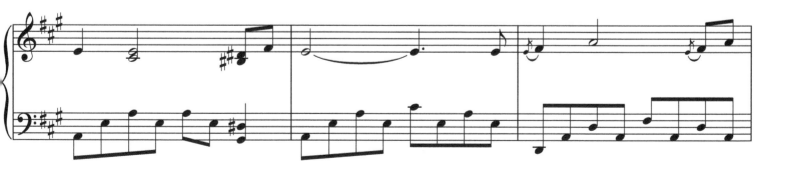

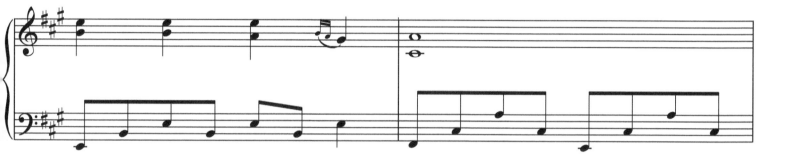

HAVE I TOLD YOU LATELY THAT I LOVE YOU

Words and Music by
SCOTT WISEMAN

Moderately fast

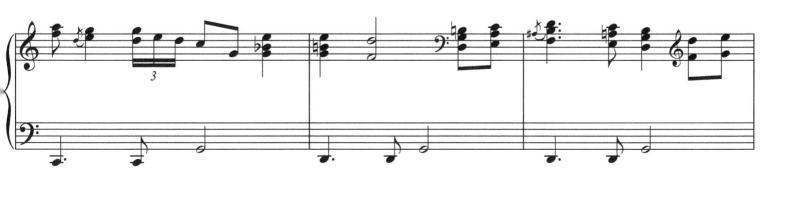

HELP ME MAKE IT
THROUGH THE NIGHT

Words and Music by
KRIS KRISTOFFERSON

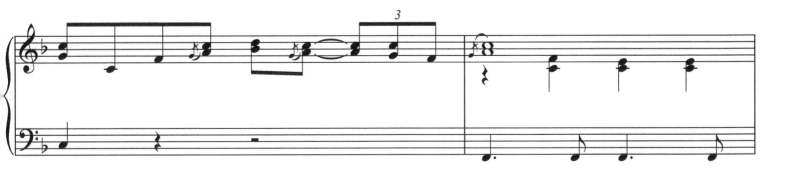

I CAN'T STOP LOVING YOU

Words and Music by
DON GIBSON

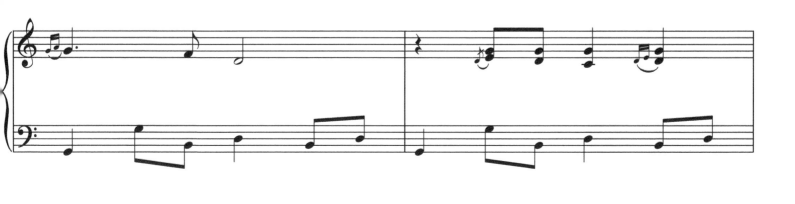

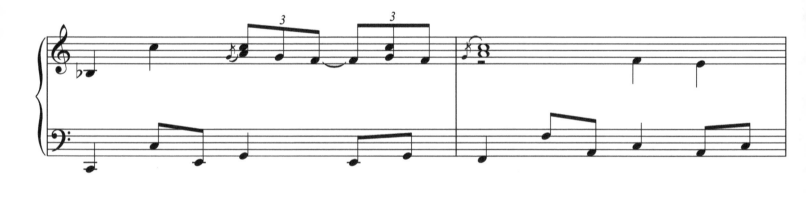

LAST DATE

By FLOYD CRAMER

Slow, relaxed feel

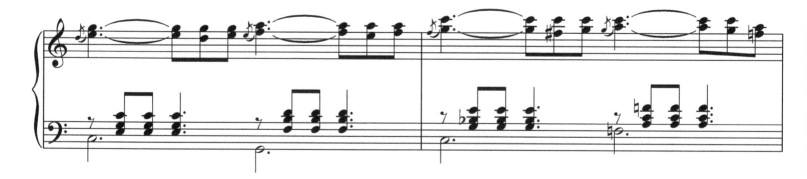

MAKE THE WORLD GO AWAY

Words and Music by
HANK COCHRAN

Moderately slow

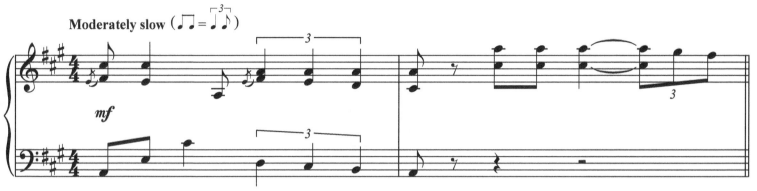

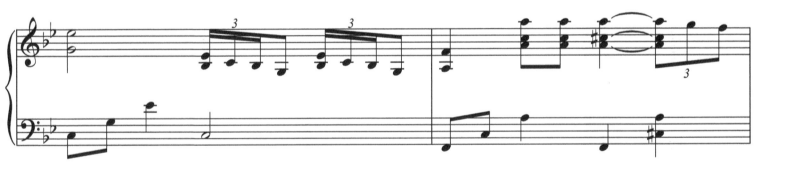

LOUISIANA MAN

Words and Music by
DOUG KERSHAW

Moderately fast

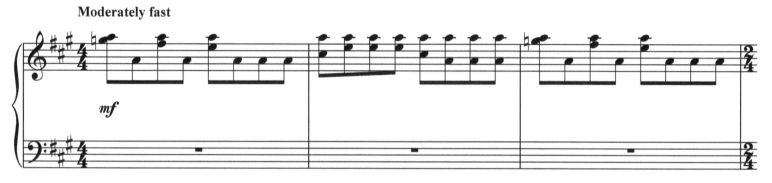

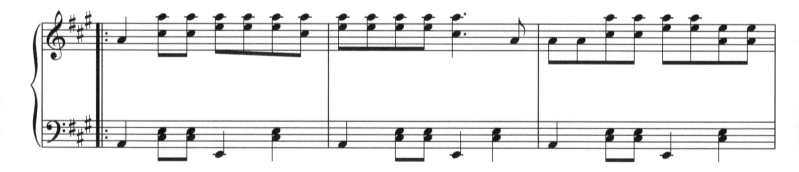

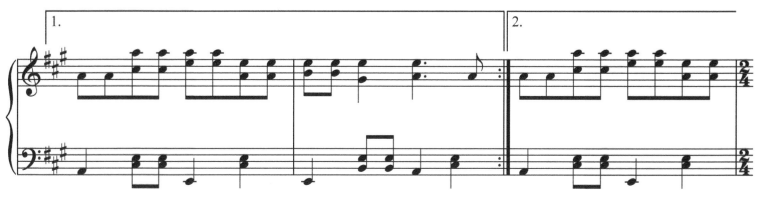

54

To Coda ⊕

D.S. al Coda

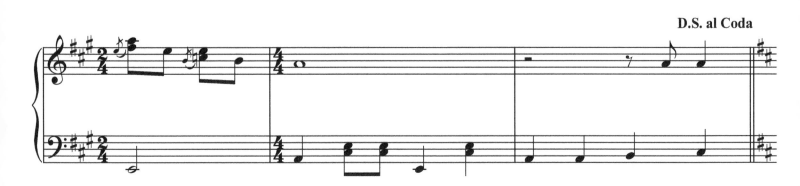

CODA

rit.

MAKING BELIEVE

Words and Music by
JIMMY WORK

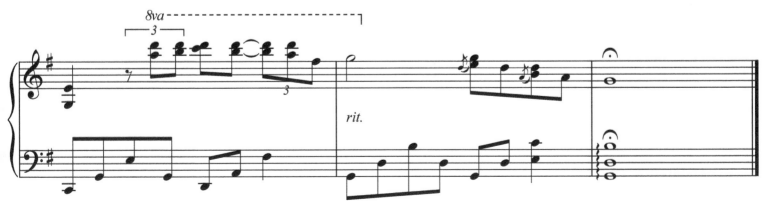

OH, LONESOME ME

Words and Music by
DON GIBSON

Moderately bright, in 2

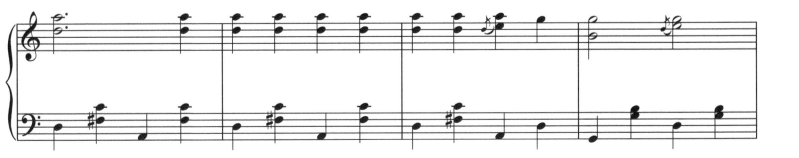

TENNESSEE WALTZ

Words and Music by REDD STEWART
and PEE WEE KING

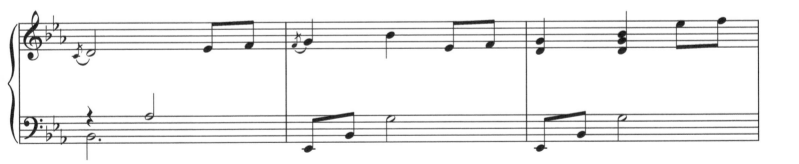

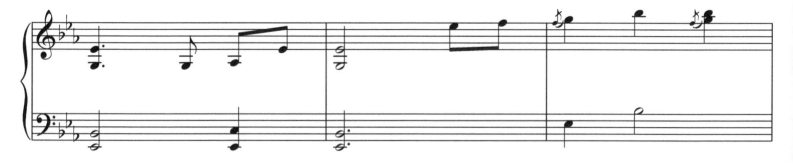

ROOM FULL OF ROSES

Words and Music by
TIM SPENCER

rit.

WALKING THE FLOOR OVER YOU

Words and Music by
ERNEST TUBB

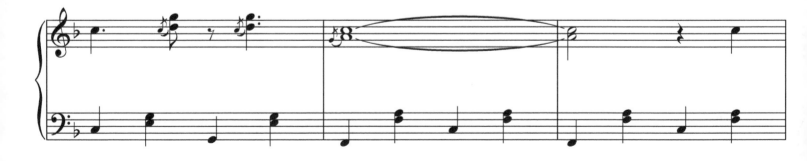

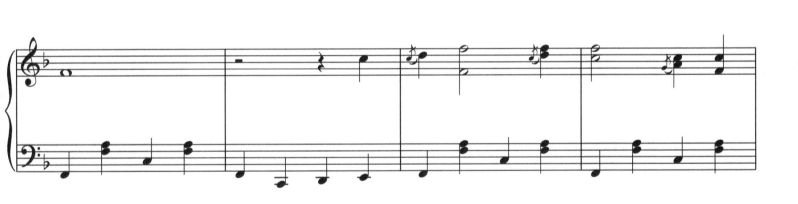

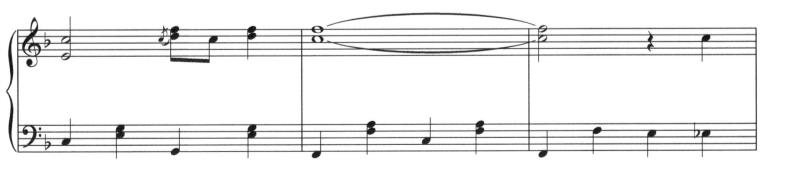

YOUR CHEATIN' HEART

Words and Music by
HANK WILLIAMS

TODAY I STARTED
LOVING YOU AGAIN

Words and Music by MERLE HAGGARD
and BONNIE OWENS

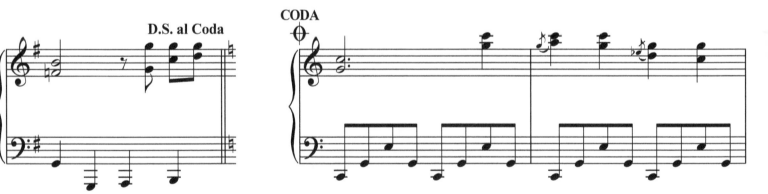

YOUR FAVORITE MUSIC
ARRANGED FOR PIANO SOLO

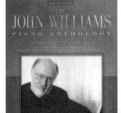

ARTIST, COMPOSER, TV & MOVIE SONGBOOKS

Adele for Piano Solo
00307585................................$17.99

The Beatles Piano Solo
00294023................................$17.99

A Charlie Brown Christmas
00313176................................$17.99

Paul Cardall – The Hymns Collection
00295925................................$24.99

Coldplay for Piano Solo
00307637................................$17.99

Selections from Final Fantasy
00148699................................$19.99

Alexis Ffrench – The Sheet Music Collection
00345258................................$19.99

Game of Thrones
00199166................................$19.99

Hamilton
00354612................................$19.99

Hillsong Worship Favorites
00303164................................$14.99

How to Train Your Dragon
00138210................................$22.99

Elton John Collection
00306040................................$24.99

La La Land
00283691................................$14.99

John Legend Collection
00233195................................$17.99

Les Misérables
00290271................................$19.99

Little Women
00338470................................$19.99

Outlander: The Series
00254460................................$19.99

The Peanuts® Illustrated Songbook
00313178................................$29.99

Astor Piazzolla – Piano Collection
00285510................................$19.99

Pirates of the Caribbean – Curse of the Black Pearl
00313256................................$19.99

Pride & Prejudice
00123854................................$17.99

Queen
00289784................................$19.99

John Williams Anthology
00194555................................$24.99

George Winston Piano Solos
00306822................................$22.99

MIXED COLLECTIONS

Beautiful Piano Instrumentals
00149926................................$16.99

Best Jazz Piano Solos Ever
00312079................................$24.99

Best Piano Solos Ever
00242928................................$19.99

Big Book of Classical Music
00310508................................$24.99

Big Book of Ragtime Piano
00311749................................$22.99

Christmas Medleys
00350572................................$16.99

Disney Medleys
00242588................................$17.99

Disney Piano Solos
00313128................................$17.99

Favorite Pop Piano Solos
00312523................................$16.99

Great Piano Solos
00311273................................$16.99

The Greatest Video Game Music
00201767................................$19.99

Most Relaxing Songs
00233879................................$17.99

Movie Themes Budget Book
00289137................................$14.99

100 of the Most Beautiful Piano Solos Ever
00102787................................$29.99

100 Movie Songs
00102804................................$29.99

Peaceful Piano Solos
00286009................................$17.99

Piano Solos for All Occasions
00310964................................$24.99

River Flows in You & Other Eloquent Songs
00123854................................$17.99

Sunday Solos for Piano
00311272................................$17.99

Top Hits for Piano Solo
00294635................................$14.99

HAL•LEONARD®
View songlists online and order from your favorite music retailer at
halleonard.com

Prices, content, and availability subject to change without notice.

Disney characters and artwork TM & © 2021 Disney

0422
195

TOP COUNTRY HITS

Arranged for piano and voice with guitar chords.

Top Country Hits of 2019-2020

18 of the best country songs from 2019 to 2020: All to Myself • Beer Never Broke My Heart • The Bones • Even Though I'm Leaving • Girl • God's Country • I Don't Know About You • Look What God Gave Her • Miss Me More • Old Town Road (Remix) • One Man Band • One Thing Right • Prayed for You • Rainbow • Remember You Young • 10,000 Hours • What If I Never Get over You • Whiskey Glasses.

00334223..$17.99

Top Country Hits of 2018-2019

18 Hot Singles

18 of the year's hottest country hits arranged for piano, voice and guitar. Includes: Best Shot (Jimmie Allen) • Drowns the Whiskey (Jason Aldean) • Get Along (Kenny Chesney) • Hangin' On (Chris Young) • Heaven (Kane Brown) • Love Wins (Carrie Underwood) • Mercy (Brett Young) • Rich (Maren Morris) • She Got the Best of Me (Luke Combs) • Simple (Florida Georgia Line) • Up Down (Morgan Wallen feat. Florida Georgia Line) • and more.

00289814..$17.99

Top Country Hits of 2017-2018

18 of the year's top toe-tapping, twangy hits: Body like a Back Road • Broken Halos • Craving You • Dear Hate • Dirt on My Boots • Dirty Laundry • Drinkin' Problem • Fighter • Hurricane • Legends • Meant to Be • Millionaire • Yours • and more.

00267160..$17.99

Top Country Hits of 2015-2016

14 of the year's most popular country songs: Burning House (Cam) • Biscuits (Kacey Musgraves) • Girl Crush (Little Big Town) • I'm Comin' Over (Chris Young) • Let Me See You Girl (Cole Swindell) • Smoke Break (Carrie Underwood) • Strip It Down (Luke Bryan) • Take Your Time (Sam Hunt) • Traveller (Chris Stapleton) • and more.

00156297..$16.99

Top Country Hits of 2014-2015

14 of the year's most popular country songs. Includes: American Kids (Kenny Chesney) • Day Drinking (Little Big Town) • I See You (Luke Bryan) • Neon Light (Blake Shelton) • Payback (Rascal Flatts) • Shotgun Rider (Tim McGraw) • Something in the Water (Carrie Underwood) • Sunshine & Whiskey (Frankie Ballard) • Talladega (Eric Church) • and more.

00142574..$16.99

Top Country Hits of 2013-2014

15 of today's most recognizable hits from country's hottest stars, including: Carolina (Parmalee) • Cruise (Florida Georgia Line) • Drunk Last Night (Eli Young Band) • Mine Would Be You (Blake Shelton) • Southern Girl (Tim McGraw) • That's My Kind of Night (Luke Bryan) • We Were Us (Keith Urban and Miranda Lambert) • and more.

00125359..$16.99

Top Country Hits of 2012-2013

Features 15 fantastic country hits: Beer Money • Begin Again • Better Dig Two • Come Wake Me Up • Every Storm (Runs Out of Rain) • Fastest Girl in Town • Hard to Love • Kiss Tomorrow Goodbye • The One That Got Away • Over You • Red • Take a Little Ride • Til My Last Day • Wanted • We Are Never Ever Getting Back Together.

00118291..$14.99

HAL•LEONARD®

Prices, content and availability subject to change without notice.